Energizing Your Faith

Energizing Your Faith

by
Jerry Savelle

HARRISON HOUSE
Tulsa, Oklahoma

3rd Printing
Over 20,000 in Print

Energizing Your Faith
ISBN 0-89274-285-2
Copyright © 1983 by Jerry Savelle
P. O. Box 2228
Fort Worth, Texas 76113

Published by Harrison House, Inc.
P. O. Box 35035
Tulsa, Oklahoma 74153

Contents

Introduction

You may have heard messages or read books about faith and how it will work. You may have already learned that faith will move mountains and overcome the world. You may have made an attempt to act on what you have learned about exercising your faith.

But are you still struggling with your faith? Does it appear to work for everyone but you? Have you been tempted to quit?

The Apostle Paul said don't cast away your confidence. (Heb. 10:35.) But many people have done just that: they have cast away their confidence when the circumstances arose and the problem got worse. They held fast to the word of faith until trouble came, then they began to compromise.

If that has happened to you, don't worry. It's in the past now; God isn't holding it against you. You can start afresh and allow your faith to be developed to the point where you absolutely refuse to bow down before the circumstances.

The truth of God's Word that I am sharing within these pages has been an exciting revelation in my life. I challenge you to set your heart and mind now to receive from God as you read.

—Jerry Savelle

1

Energizing Your Faith

Grace to you, and peace, from God our Father and the Lord Jesus Christ. I thank my God, making mention of thee always in my prayers, hearing of thy love and faith, which thou hast toward the Lord Jesus, and toward all saints;

That the communication of thy faith may become effectual by the acknowledging of every good thing which is in you in Christ Jesus.

For we have great joy and consolation in thy love, because the bowels of the saints are refreshed by thee, brother.

Philemon 3-7

In the above verses we find the Apostle Paul commending Philemon for the way he has been so gracious and loving toward the saints of God. He is thanking Philemon for his godly behavior and for obeying the Spirit of God where the necessity of the saints was concerned.

The portion of Scripture I want particularly to deal with in this study is verse 6. This one verse is packed full of truth regarding the subject of faith.

That the communication of thy faith may become effectual by the acknowledging of every good thing which is in you in Christ Jesus.

When studying the God kind of faith, no matter how we approach it, we have to include the subject of confession, because words are the primary way in which faith is released.

In Genesis, chapter 1, when God released His faith to create the universe, we read these words: *And God said . . . .*

In Mark 11:14 Jesus *said* to the fig tree, *No man eat fruit of thee hereafter for ever.* The next morning when the disciples saw that the tree had withered from the roots, Peter said, "Master, look! The fig tree which You cursed has withered away." (v. 21.)

Jesus answered and said, *Have faith in God* (the faith of God or the God kind of faith). He was implying that it was the God kind of faith which caused the fig tree to wither from the roots.

What did Jesus do to get the tree to wither? He spoke to it. He used words; then He connected words with the God kind of faith.

Paul stated a truth to Philemon that can apply to you and me today. This truth will reveal, in particular, the reason behind the confession of our lips. Let's look at verse 6 again:

That the communication of thy faith may become effectual by the acknowledging of every good thing which is in you in Christ Jesus.

Notice the phrase, "the communication of **thy** faith." Place yourself in this verse and read it that way: "That the communication of **my** faith may become effectual by the acknowledging of every good thing which is in **me** in Christ Jesus.''

When you see the word *communication*, what do you think of? Words. When you speak words, what are you doing? Communicating.

The Greek word that is translated *communication* literally implies the exercising or releasing of faith. Paul is saying, ''That the *exercising* of your faith may become effectual . . . .''

The Greek word translated *effectual* means divinely energized, indicating that it is superhuman. Paul is showing how we can have our faith divinely energized, or energized by the Holy One.

Wouldn't you agree that Jesus' faith was divinely energized? Not one time during His ministry did Jesus ever sense a lack of faith. Not once did He say, ''Oh, dear God, I sure hope I have enough faith this time!'' He always knew His faith would work. He never questioned the ability of God that was working through Him. **His faith was divinely energized!**

Well, praise God, our faith can become divinely energized, too! Paul goes on to tell us how it's done.

2
Acknowledge
The Good Things

I like the way the Spirit of God speaks to us. He never says, "If you had faith, you could do anything; but don't get your hopes up too high." He always tells us what faith will do, then He tells us how to do it. He says in Philemon 6: *That the communication of thy faith may become effectual **by the acknowledging of every good thing which is in you in Christ Jesus.***

When I read this verse, I picture God asking me this question: "Jerry, how would you like to have your faith divinely energized? If so, then here is how you do it." He is saying that our faith can become divinely energized, but we have to do something: acknowledge the things He has instructed us to acknowledge.

Let's say you are walking down the street when someone says, "Hello." To acknowledge that person, you could wave or smile; but the predominant way is by speaking words. To acknowledge literally means to speak.

"That your faith may become *divinely energized* by the acknowledging." The closest word in the Greek to the meaning of the word *acknowledging* is the word *confessing*. Both of these involve speaking. Let's read it again:

"That the exercising of your faith may become *divinely energized* by the *confessing* of every good thing which is in you in Christ Jesus."

If we expect our faith to be divinely energized, we have to follow God's instructions. He didn't say, ". . . by the acknowledging of every bad, evil, or

16

sad thing." In fact, He didn't stop with *every good thing*. He said, . . . *by the acknowledging of every good thing which is in you in Christ Jesus.* Your faith will become divinely energized as you confess what you are, who you are, and what belongs to you in Christ Jesus. We are to acknowledge every good thing that Jesus has done for us through His work at Calvary.

In the past, we have made operating in the God kind of faith difficult and hard. But as we have already seen from Mark, chapter 11, Jesus said, "Have the God kind of faith." If He said we could have it, there must be a way to get it.

The Gospel is simple. It is our religious, traditional thinking and worldly programming that has kept us from receiving all that God has for us in His Word.

When I first started reading the Word of God, I had a terrible time! I would become discouraged and complain that I couldn't understand it.

Then the Lord began to show me that I was acknowledging the wrong things. So I started finding Scripture verses about how the Spirit of Truth is in me and He will teach me all things and bring all things to my remembrance. I learned that I have the mind of Christ.

Then I started acknowledging what the Word said—confessing what the Bible had to say, instead of what my mind had to say. I would proclaim in faith, ''In the name of Jesus, I *can* understand the Word of God, because I have the mind of Christ.''

The first few times I said it, my head screamed, ''You can't understand!'' But I continued to say it. Before long I began to believe it!

I would confess Philippians 4:19 over and over: ''My God supplies all my need according to His riches in glory by Christ Jesus.'' It didn't look like God was meeting all my needs, but I said it so much that it started forming an

18

image inside me. I could see my needs being met.

When you read the Bible, put aside your religious eyeglasses. Put aside everything you *think* the Bible says and read what it actually says. Then meditate on it; think about it; dwell on it. Acknowledge what the Bible says about you—not what people say, or what your body says, or what your bankbook says. Start confessing and acknowledging the good things that are in you in Christ Jesus. As you do, your faith will become divinely energized and work for you the way Jesus' faith works for Him.

James 1:17 says, *Every good gift and every perfect gift is from above, and cometh down from the Father of lights, with whom is no variableness, neither shadow of turning.*

Every good thing comes from the Father above, and you are to acknowledge every good thing which is in you in Christ Jesus. You are to confess what the Word says about you and all that Jesus did for you at Calvary.

What are some of the good things that are in you in Christ Jesus? Here are just a few:

You are redeemed from the curse of the Law. (Gal. 3:13.)

You are blessed with all spiritual blessings. (Eph. 1:3.)

You have been made to sit with Him in heavenly places. (Eph. 2:6.)

He bore your sicknesses and carried your diseases. (Matt. 8:17.)

You lay your hands on the sick and they recover. (Mark 16:18.)

Your God supplies all your need according to His riches in glory by Christ Jesus. (Phil. 4:19.)

You have been delivered out of the power of darkness and translated into the Kingdom of His dear Son. (Col. 1:13.)

You can receive these promises as your own because you are in Christ Jesus. When you acknowledge these good things in Christ Jesus, your faith will become divinely energized.

This is what I do continually as I prepare to preach. I walk the floor of my room, acknowledging all the good things and confessing all that I am in Christ Jesus. By the time I get to the service, my faith is divinely energized and I expect things to happen: souls to be saved, the sick to be healed, demonic spirits to flee at the name of Jesus.

Some people think that acknowledging what God says is ignoring problems, but it isn't. I don't ignore my problems; I just don't acknowledge them. There is a difference.

I don't ignore the existence of sickness; but I refuse to acknowledge its right to exist in my body.

I don't ignore the problem of inflation; but I don't acknowledge its right to affect my life. If the price of a loaf of bread went to $5.95, I wouldn't worry and say, "Oh, dear God, what are we going to do?" I would simply acknowledge the *good* thing in me in Christ Jesus: that my God supplies all my need according to His riches in glory by Christ Jesus.

The good thing in me in Christ Jesus is that I am the righteousness of God. (2 Cor. 5:21.) Psalm 37:25 says, *I have been young, and now am old; yet have I not seen the righteous forsaken, nor his seed begging bread.*

Somebody may say, "But what about the devil? Don't you have trouble with him?"

Don't ever think the devil takes this sitting still. He challenges me daily— and daily he gets defeated. I have had numerous opportunities to fall flat on my face. Many times I have wanted to scream, "Dear God, take me out of here! I can't stand it anymore!" But that would be acknowledging the wrong thing.

There were times when the Apostle Paul was in trouble. He described some of these in the eleventh chapter of his second letter to the Corinthians:

. . . in labours more abundant, in stripes above measure, in prisons more frequent, in deaths oft. Of the Jews five times received I forty stripes save one.

Thrice was I beaten with rods, once was I stoned, thrice I suffered shipwreck, a night and a day I have been in the deep;

In journeyings often, in perils of waters, in perils of robbers, in perils by mine own countrymen, in perils by the heathen, in perils in the city, in perils in the wilderness, in perils of the sea, in perils among false brethren;

In weariness and painfulness, in watchings often, in hunger and thirst, in fastings often, in cold and nakedness (vv. 23-27).

In 2 Corinthians 4:8,9 he wrote: *We are troubled on every side, yet not distressed; we are perplexed, but not in despair; persecuted, but not forsaken; cast down, but not destroyed.* In verse 17, he called these experiences "light affliction."

Paul lived through an enormous amount of persecutions and afflictions, but he wasn't moved by them. He didn't allow them to rule his life.

In 2 Timothy 4:6,7 he wrote: *For I am now ready to be offered, and the time of my departure is at hand. I have fought a good fight, I have finished my course, I have kept the faith.* Through all of his problems, he kept right on acknowledging that he was fully persuaded that God was able to deliver him.

In spite of all that happened to discourage Paul, he absolutely refused to bow down. He didn't ignore problems; he just kept acknowledging the good things in him in Christ Jesus. No wonder his faith was so highly developed!

If you want your faith highly developed and divinely energized, then do what Paul did: acknowledge every good thing that is in you in Christ Jesus. Don't ignore the problems; but at the same time, don't acknowledge their dominance in your life. Instead, acknowledge the dominance of Jesus and His Word.

3

Logos and Rhema

In the Greek, there are two words that refer to God's Word: *logos* and *rhema*. Many scholars have thought these two words meant the same thing, but they are distinctively different. One Scripture verse is a part of the *logos* of God; but when quoted by a believer, it becomes the *rhema* of God.

Logos is the sum total of all the expressions or sayings of God. The Bible—Genesis to Revelation—is the *logos* of God.

In John 1:1 we read, *In the beginning was the Word, and the Word was with God, and the Word was God.* The Greek word used here is *logos*. "In the beginning was the *logos*, and the *logos* was with God, and the *logos* was God."

In Matthew 4:1-4 Jesus used the word *rhema*.

Then was Jesus led up of the Spirit into the wilderness to be tempted of the devil.

And when he had fasted forty days and forty nights, he was afterward an hungred.

And when the tempter came to him, he said, If thou be the Son of God, command that these stones be made bread.

But he answered and said, It is written, Man shall not live by bread alone, but by every word **(rhema)** *that proceedeth out of the mouth of God.*

Jesus didn't stand before the devil and throw the whole *logos* of God at him. He spoke and acknowledged only the portion of God's Word He needed in that particular situation. He spoke the *rhema* of God. He took a singular expression from the sum total of the sayings of God. That one saying fit the occasion and was more than enough to defeat the devil.

When the devil came back to tempt Him again, what did Jesus do? He took another *rhema*. He said, *It is written . . .*, and quoted another verse of Scripture. (v. 7.) He took an explicit Scripture verse that fit the occasion and spoke it in faith at the devil.

Let's look now at Ephesians, chapter 6. Here the Apostle Paul is describing the Christian's warfare with the devil and the spiritual weapons that God has put at our disposal. In verses 10-17 we read:

Finally, my brethren, be strong in the Lord, and in the power of his might.

Put on the whole armour of God, that ye may be able to stand against the wiles of the devil.

For we wrestle not against flesh and blood, but against principalities, against powers, against the rulers of the darkness of this world, against spiritual wickedness in high places.

Wherefore take unto you the whole armour of God, that ye may be able to withstand in the evil day, and having done all, to stand.

Stand therefore, having your loins girt about with truth, and having on the breastplate of righteousness; and your feet shod with the preparation of the gospel of peace;

Above all, taking the shield of faith, wherewith ye shall be able to quench all the fiery darts of the wicked. And take the helmet of salvation, and the sword of the Spirit, which is the word of God.

In this last verse the Greek word used is *rhema*, not *logos*. . . . *and the sword of the Spirit, which is the* **rhema** *of God.*

As a believer, you are involved in a warfare. Demonic forces are trying their best to keep you from receiving the answers to your prayers. Paul says you are to put on the whole armor of God. You are to take the shield of faith and the sword of the Spirit—the Word of God.

This is not a picture of a believer throwing the whole Bible at the devil. It is a picture of a believer taking explicit Scripture verses that fit the occasion and speaking them out his mouth like rapid fire from a machine gun. No wonder James 4:7 says, *Resist the devil, and he will flee from you.* One translation says he will run in stark terror.

This is exactly the way Jesus stood against Satan—not in His own power, but under the power of the *rhema* of God. He took particular Scripture verses that fit the occasion and spoke them out His mouth. His faith was divinely energized, so the devil had to flee.

Do you remember what it was like when you first heard the Word concerning healing? Remember how excited you were when the truth of 1 Peter 2:24

became real to you—that by His stripes you were healed?

When you started acknowledging that truth, your faith grew to an enormous level. But what happened later? The devil came to steal the Word and prove to you that you couldn't be healed. That's what Jesus said he would do. After you have heard the Word, Satan will come immediately to steal the Word that was sown in your heart. (Mark 4:15.) This is where your faith will either become divinely energized or lay dormant.

When the devil comes to steal the Word from your heart, you will acknowledge something. Acknowledge the wrong thing, and your faith will lay dormant and stagnant. Acknowledge the right thing, and your faith will be divinely energized. When the pressure is on, you must acknowledge—more than ever before—the good thing which is in you in Christ Jesus.

When your body feels the worst, you must acknowledge what God's Word says: "By His stripes I am healed." Say that often enough and it will get into your heart in abundance. Then you will delight in saying it. You will begin to say it before sickness comes, and that Word will keep sickness away from you.

Don't wait until you get sick to confess God's healing power in your body. Get up in the morning when you are feeling well and say with thanksgiving to God: "By His stripes, I am healed." That will put you on the road to divine health.

Don't wait until the pressure is on to act on the Word. It is harder to confess you are healed when you feel bad than when you feel good. Acknowledge the good things continually.

Jesus spoke the *rhema* of God, and it divinely energized His faith. He acknowledged what the Word said about His situation. He didn't ignore the problem; He just looked beyond it and acknowledged the truth of God's Word.

Let's look again at Ephesians 6:10-17, this time from *The New Testament in Modern English* by J. B. Phillips:

"In conclusion be strong—not in yourselves but in the Lord, in the power of his boundless strength. Put on God's complete armour so that you can successfully resist all the devil's craftiness. For our fight is not against any physical enemy: it is against organizations and powers that are spiritual. We are up against the unseen power that controls this dark world, and spiritual agents from the very headquarters of evil.

"Therefore you must wear the whole armour of God that you may be able to resist evil in its day of power, and that even when you have fought to a standstill you may still stand your ground.

34

"Take your stand then with truth as your belt, integrity your breastplate, the gospel of peace firmly on your feet, salvation as your helmet and in your hand the sword of the Spirit, the Word of God.

"Above all be sure you take faith as your shield, for it can quench every burning missile the enemy hurls at you."

We are not up against seen powers, but against the unseen spiritual agents from the very headquarters of hell. Therefore, you must wear the whole armor of God; you must take the shield of faith, which can quench every burning missile that the enemy hurls at you, and the sword of the Spirit, which is the Word of God.

The Apostle Paul is describing a person in actual battle with Satan. When you are in a battle with satanic forces, God doesn't expect you to quote the entire *logos* as you take the Sword of the Spirit. All you have to do to stop

Satan's attack is acknowledge the good thing which is in you in Christ Jesus.

The moment an attack comes, acknowledge explicit, singular sayings of God that fit the occasion. If sickness is attacking you, take the *rhema* of God concerning healing and use it as a sword in combat against your symptoms. If finances are your problem, take the *rhema* of God that pertains to financial prosperity and stand against that attack of Satan.

As Phillips says, ". . . even when you have fought to a standstill you may still stand your ground."

In war after war, there have been standstill situations. But eventually somebody compromised and the standstill was broken. One side will always back down during a standstill, and the other side will take the advantage. It may take some time, but the compromise will come.

Let me share a little secret with you: It is Satan's nature to compromise. But according to *The Amplified Bible*, a believer should become "the *uncompromisingly* righteous."

When you have released your faith against the problem and have spoken the *rhema* of God pertaining to the situation, then stand your ground and refuse to listen to the devil's lies. Know that even when you have fought to a standstill, you can still stand your ground. You don't have to compromise. Just speak the *rhema* and let the Word fight its own fight. Rejoice like the Psalmist, knowing that God will maintain your right and your cause. (Ps. 9:4.)

4

Taming Your Tongue

O generation of vipers, how can ye, being evil, speak good things? for out of the abundance of the heart the mouth speaketh.

A good man out of the good treasure of the heart bringeth forth good things: and an evil man out of the evil treasure bringeth forth evil things.

But I say unto you, That every idle word that men shall speak, they shall give account thereof in the day of judgment.

For by thy words thou shalt be justified, and by thy words thou shalt be condemned.
Matthew 12:34-37

Jesus said that out of the abundance of a man's heart, his mouth will speak, and out of the good treasure of a good man's heart, good things will come to pass.

When you continue to acknowledge the good things God says about your circumstances and situations, then good things will come to pass. When you continue to acknowledge bad things in your life, then bad things will come to pass.

If you are presently experiencing some bad situations, the first thing you should do is check up on your vocabulary. Your problem may lie with that little thing in your mouth called the tongue.

James 3:2 says, *For in many things we offend all. If any man offend not in word, the same is a perfect man, and able also to bridle the whole body.* If a person can learn to take control of his tongue, he can control his whole body. This indicates to me that most of the problems a person has with his body stem from the kind of words he speaks.

James gives some illustrations so we can see how this works.

In verse 3 he writes: *Behold* (or look and see), *we put bits in the horses' mouths, that they may obey us; and we turn about their whole body*. He is saying that by putting a small piece of metal in a horse's mouth, we can control the horse and make it do what we want.

Here is the parallel he is drawing: In the same manner that you control a horse with the bit in its mouth, you can learn to control your whole body by taming your tongue.

Verse 4 reads: *Behold also the ships, which though they be so great, and are driven of fierce winds, yet are they turned about with a very small helm, whithersoever the governor listeth*. Again we see a parallel, this time using the helm of a ship.

The helm is a steering device that controls the rudder of a ship. Though the rudder is not nearly the size of the ship, it can change the course of that ship. Your tongue is tiny in comparison to the size of your body, but the words spoken by your tongue will change the course of your life. You can actually control the storms of your life by learning to tame your tongue and talk God's Word.

Even so the tongue is a little member, and boasteth great things. Behold, how great a matter a little fire kindleth! (v. 5). Words act as kindling wood to a fire. Talking negatively, a little here and a little there, is just like putting pine knots in a fireplace. A big log won't burn just by putting a match to it. You need to have some kindling—wood shavings and pine knots. Put kindling under that log and set it on fire. Before long, the log will be blazing.

That is exactly what happens when you talk anything other than the good things that are in you in Christ Jesus. Your words act like kindling wood to a fire. Somewhere down the road they will consume you.

*The tongue is a fire, a world of iniquity:
so is the tongue among our members, that it
defileth the whole body, and setteth on fire
the course of nature; and it is set on fire of
hell* (v. 6). Your tongue sets in motion
the cycle of your life. Your life today is
the sum total of the words you have
been speaking. If you don't like what
you are, change your vocabulary.

When you talk what God's Word
says, acknowledging the good thing
which is in you in Christ Jesus, the
Apostle and High Priest of your
confession, Jesus Christ, will back your
words. (Heb. 3:1.) He will agree with
you and see that it comes to pass.

Words can change your eternal
destiny. That is why God placed such a
high premium on words. The basic
requirement for becoming a Christian
involves speaking right words: *That if
thou shalt confess with thy mouth the Lord
Jesus, and shalt believe in thine heart that
God hath raised him from the dead, thou
shalt be saved* (Rom. 10:9).

Because of the words I spoke a number of years ago, confessing faith in Jesus as Lord and proclaiming that God had raised Him from the dead, I am no longer bound for hell. Those words changed my destiny.

Think about this: If words can change my eternal destiny and send me to heaven instead of hell, is it unreasonable to say that words can change my body and the physical circumstances of my life? If words can change my destiny, they can change anything. There is power in words.

God has put within you His kind of faith, a faith that will become either stagnant or divinely energized. Only you can determine which it will be.

God has given you the method by which your faith can be divinely energized. That method is found in Philemon 6, as we have already quoted: the acknowledging of every good thing which is in you in Christ Jesus. As long as you continue to acknowledge the problems, you will never overcome them. If you will say the same thing about your problems and circumstances that God says about them, your faith will be energized and will enable you to overcome the world.

Psalm 103:20 says the angels of God excel in strength and do His commandments, hearkening unto the voice of His Word. When you talk God's Word, the angels come on the scene to see that what you say comes to pass.

Guess who comes on the scene when you aren't talking the Word? Satan's gang! They will try to make the negative things you say come to pass. All the more reason to watch what you say and make the words of your mouth be a continuous confession of the goodness of God at work in your life.

If a man can bridle his tongue, he can bridle his whole body. If he can tame his tongue, he can change his eternal destiny and stop the destruction that the storms of life can bring.

But James 3:7,8 seems to put a negative tone on this business of taming the tongue:

For every kind of beasts, and of birds, and of serpents, and of things in the sea, is tamed, and hath been tamed of mankind:

But the tongue can no man tame; it is an unruly evil, full of deadly poison.

Does this mean we have to live in this miserable state, because we can never tame our tongues? No, that's not what it means.

James is saying that God has given to man the natural ability to tame wild animals, but the tongue cannot be tamed by that same natural ability. It takes the supernatural power of God to tame the tongue.

If you want your tongue to be tamed, you must submit your vocabulary to the supernatural power of God. The only way you can do that is by talking God's Word. When you do, the power and anointing that is in God's

Word will tame your tongue. There will come a time when you refuse to say anything contrary to the truth in God's Word.

This doesn't come overnight. It takes time and a heartfelt decision on your part. You will have to say, "In the name of Jesus, I refuse to speak or acknowledge anything other than the good things which are in me in Christ Jesus."

Proverbs 4:24 refers to "a froward mouth." *Put away from thee a froward mouth, and perverse lips put far from thee.* A froward mouth is an uncontrollable mouth—one that talks what it wants to talk, regardless of what God's Word says.

How do you put away a froward mouth? . . . *attend to my words; incline thine ear unto my sayings. Let them not depart from thine eyes; keep them in the midst of thine heart* (Prov. 4:20,21).

47

Give your total attention to the Word of God. Acknowledge the Word instead of the problem. Quit talking the problem and start talking the answer—God's Word.

The next time you have an opportunity to get depressed because of the way your circumstances look, do this: Get your Bible, open it, and begin to quote it out loud. Say what God's Word says about you. If you don't know enough of the Word to apply it to your particular problem, just start reading any of the epistles of Paul. If you read long enough, you will find something that pertains to your problem. For instance, Colossians 1:12,13 says:

Giving thanks unto the Father . . . Who hath delivered us from the power of darkness, and hath translated us into the kingdom of his dear Son.

According to Ephesians 1:3, you are blessed *with all spiritual blessings in heavenly places in Christ.*

Paul's prayer for the Church was that God give us the *spirit of wisdom and revelation in the knowledge of him* (Eph. 1:17). In Ephesians 2:10 he wrote, *We are his workmanship, created in Christ Jesus unto good works.*

As you begin to acknowledge what the Word says, it will energize your faith and at the same time enable you to bring your tongue under control. The final result then is this: **If you can control your tongue, you can control your body and the circumstances of your entire life.**

To understand how powerful words are, let's get an illustration from the Word of God. Let's find somebody who acknowledged the wrong things and see what happened to his faith.

You have probably heard a few sermons on the Book of Job. If you will, just forget them for the moment. I want to show you from God's Word that Job's problem was **not** God.

I'm convinced that the book of Job, if preached correctly, will not inspire fear, sadness, sorrow, or grief, but will do exactly what every other book in the Bible is designed to do: create faith.

Wrong Words Are Forcible

The Bible says that Job was the richest man in all the East. (Job 1:3.) According to Deuteronomy 8:18, it is God Who gives the power to get wealth. God made Job rich, then built a hedge around him. But Satan came on the scene and began his usual maneuvers. Jesus later described the devil as a thief who comes to kill, steal, and destroy. (John 10:10.)

Satan's operation was set in motion by the words of Job's mouth. When destruction had come to his family and possessions, Job said: *For the thing which I greatly feared has come upon me, and that which I was afraid of is come unto me. I was not in safety, neither had I rest, neither was I quiet; yet trouble came* (Job 3:25,26).

50

Notice he said, . . . *the thing which I greatly feared* . . . . As we have discovered in this study, faith activates God, and that faith is released from the heart predominately by words.

Fear is the opposite force of faith. If faith is released by words, then fear can be released by words. Fear activates Satan the same way faith activates God. Job began to see the thing he so greatly feared come upon him.

If you have fear in your heart, you will speak that fear. If you have faith in your heart, you will speak that faith. There is no way around it. What you believe in your heart, you will speak with your mouth. (Matt. 12:34.)

In order for Satan to be activated, Job had to release that fear out of his heart by speaking it. He **said**, . . . *the thing which I greatly feared has come upon me.* Job had been fearing destruction for a long time; and because he was speaking his fear, it activated Satan and brought destruction.

51

Job 1:21 tells us what the man had been thinking about and what he had been saying: *Naked came I out of my mother's womb, and naked shall I return thither: the Lord gave, and the Lord hath taken away . . . .*

The thing Job feared was losing all his possessions. What he was saying was, ''When I came into this world, I didn't have anything, and it's for sure that when I leave, I'll have nothing.''

The first thing that came out of his mouth was the first sign of the cause of his destruction. It indicated what he had been talking all the time.

Job didn't know any better than to say, *The Lord gave, and the Lord hath taken away.* It is true that Job made this statement, but what he said was not a statement of truth.

Again, I refer to Jesus' words in John 10:10: *The thief cometh not, but for to steal, and to kill, and to destroy: I am come that*

*they might have life, and that they might
have it more abundantly.*

God does not give, then take away.
If He did, then the other Scripture
verses that show Him as a God Who
never changes would not be true. God
is not double-minded. The Bible says
that there is no variableness or shadow
of turning in Him. (James 1:17.) If the
Lord gives, He is not going to take
away.

How Forcible Are Right Words!

Job didn't know what to do, so he
just associated his problems with God.
Later on he began to recognize where
he made his mistake. He realized,
"Hey, my tongue has gotten me into
trouble. That which I've so greatly
feared, I've been talking; and what I've
been talking has brought all this
destruction."

Job's problem was only an inch from
his nose—his tongue! He said some
things he should not have said, and

53

destruction was the result. He experienced the force of wrong words.

Job recognized what his problem was when he said, *How forcible are right words!* (Job 6:25). The Bible says God turned the captivity of Job. (Job 42:10.)

Learn from Job and don't make his mistakes. That is why the Book of Job is in the Bible. If we can learn from the things Job experienced, we won't have to go through those same things ourselves. Just take his word for it: Right words **are** forcible!

5

Speak Right Words

Thank God for the writings of Solomon! He knew the power of words. In Proverbs 18:21, he wrote:

Death and life are in the power of the tongue: and they that love it shall eat the fruit thereof.

Let's look at some scriptures that pertain to *death* being in the tongue:

The wicked is snared by the transgression of his lips (Prov. 12:13).

. . . the mouth of the foolish is near destruction (Prov. 10:14).

. . . violence covereth the mouth of the wicked (Prov. 10:11).

. . . he that openeth wide his lips shall have destruction (Prov. 13:3).

... *but perverseness* (in the tongue) *is a breach in the spirit* (Prov. 15:4).

A fool's mouth is his destruction, and his lips are the snare of his soul (Prov. 18:7).

Now let's look at some scriptures under the category of *life* being in the tongue:

The mouth of a righteous man is a well of life (Prov. 10:11).

... *he that refraineth his lips is wise* (Prov. 10:19).

The tongue of the just is as choice silver (Prov. 10:20).

... *the mouth of the upright shall deliver them* (Prov. 12:6).

... *the tongue of the wise is health* (Prov. 12:18).

He that keepeth his mouth keepeth his life (Prov. 13:3).

A wholesome tongue is a tree of life (Prov. 15:4).

With this much evidence from the Word of God, there is no doubt to me that there is enormous power in the words we speak.

Life—and living it the way God intends—is wrapped up in what we say. As Job put it: *How forcible are right words!* (Job 6:25). The word *forcible* means having the ability to overcome, influence, control, or persuade. We can see this in the ministry of Jesus. His words overcame sickness and disease in the lives of people wherever He preached.

How forcible are right words! What are "right words"? The Wisdom of God tells us in the eighth chapter of Proverbs:

Doth not wisdom cry? and understanding put forth her voice?

She standeth in the top of high places, by the way in the places of the paths.

She crieth at the gates, at the entry of the city, at the coming in at the doors.

Unto you, O men, I call; and my voice is to the sons of men.

O ye simple, understand wisdom: and, ye fools, be ye of an understanding heart.

Hear: for I will speak of excellent things; and the opening of my lips shall be right things.

For my mouth shall speak truth; and wickedness is an abomination to my lips.

All the words of my mouth are in righteousness; there is nothing froward or perverse in them.

They are all plain to him that understandeth, and right to them that find knowledge (vv. 1-9).

Here we see the Wisdom of God crying out, ''I am right words! I am the truth! I, Wisdom (the Word of God), say this to you: Only the things which I speak are excellent things. The opening of my lips shall be right things.''

The right words are God's words. As Job says, *How forcible are right words!* If right words have the ability to control, influence, persuade, and overcome, then you should speak right words. You can always be assured of speaking the right words when you speak God's Word.

Listen to what God says about His Word:

"For the Word that God speaks is alive and full of power—making it active, operative, energizing and effective" (Heb. 4:12, AMP).

"I am alert and active, watching over My word to perform it" (Jer. 1:12, AMP).

"For I am the Lord; I will speak, and the word that I shall speak shall be performed" (Ezek. 12:25, AMP).

If you follow God's instructions—incline your ear to His sayings and speak the right words—the words that you speak *shall* come to pass!

You can change your entire life—finances, health, family, job, everything—by speaking the right words. Jesus is the Apostle and High Priest of your confession. When you say things that He can agree with, He will see that they come to pass.

Confession

In the name of Jesus, I am a believer. I believe God's Word. I am what the Word says I am. I have what the Word says I have. I can do what the Word says I can do.

In Jesus' name, I render ineffective every negative word I have spoken, every word that has been contrary to the truth of God's Word.

From this moment forward, I will acknowledge the good things that are in me in Christ Jesus. I'm saying it now: Out of the good treasure of my heart, only good things will come to pass.

I am the righteousness of God, a new creation, an heir of God, and a joint-heir with Jesus. I've been delivered from the power of darkness and translated into the Kingdom of God's dear Son.

I've been redeemed by the blood of the Lamb—redeemed from the curse of the Law; redeemed from sickness and disease, poverty and death.

I can do all things through Christ Who strengthens me. I am more than a conqueror. He never leaves me nor forsakes me. Because the Greater One dwells within me, I can overcome every situation. The faith of God resides within me, and through it I have the victory that overcomes the world.

I thank You, Father, that I can have all these things. I believe it in my heart. I have released it with my mouth. So be it. It will surely come to pass, in Jesus' name.

Jerry Savelle, noted author, evangelist, and Bible teacher, shares the uncompromising Word of God with a power and authority that is exciting, but with a love that delivers the message directly to the heart. His down-  to-earth approach and dynamic illustrations clearly present the absolute authority of God's Word.

At age 12 as Jerry was watching the healing ministry of Oral Roberts on television, God spoke to his heart and called him into the ministry. Several years later, on February 11, 1969, Jerry made Jesus Christ the Lord of his life. Since then, he has been moving in the light of God's calling on his life. Prior to entering his own ministry, Jerry was an associate minister with Kenneth Copeland Evangelistic Association.

The scope of Jerry Savelle Ministries is far reaching. Besides traveling throughout the United States, Canada, and other parts of the world, Jerry conducts a daily radio program, ''Adventures In Faith.''

The anointing of God upon Jerry's life is powerful, and people are set free as the Word goes forth unhindered.

For a complete list of tapes and books by Jerry Savelle,
write

Jerry Savelle Ministries
P.O. Box 2228 • Fort Worth, TX 76113